Original Title: 101 STRANGE BUT TRUE CYCLING
FACTS

©101 STRANGE BUT TRUE CYCLING FACTS, Carlos
Martínez Cerdá and Victor Martínez Cerdá, 2023

Authors: Victor Martínez Cerdá and Carlos Martínez
Cerdá (V&C Brothers)

© Cover and illustrations: V&C Brothers

Layout and design: V&C Brothers

101
STRANGE BUT TRUE
CYCLING FACTS

1

The evolution of bicycles.

Cycling as a sport was first introduced in the early 1800s and quickly became very popular.

There are records of the oldest basic design of a bicycle dating back to 1493, when Gian Giacomo Caprotti outlined the idea.

However, the first bicycle recognized as such was created by German Karl von Drais in 1817.

At that time, it was called a balance bicycle.

About 20 years later, in 1865, a locksmith named Ernest Michaux decided to add two pedals to the front wheel directly on its axis, to facilitate the machine's progress.

Two years later, Michaux added brakes to the front wheel, to stop the machine more easily.

Shortly thereafter, the chain drive system was installed on the rear wheel.

Over time, the bicycle has evolved into what is now known worldwide.

2

The beginnings of cycling.

In 1868, the first documented
bicycle race was held.

Cyclists traveled 1,200 meters in the
Saint-Cloud Park in Paris.

In the United States, bicycles were incredibly
popular in the early 1900s.

The oldest bicycle racing club, the St. Louis
Cycling Club, was established in 1887
and continues to sponsor races
and other events today.

However, starting in 1920, the practice of
cycling gradually faded due to the
development of the automobile.

The beginning of the 21st century saw a
resurgence of the bicycle as a substitute for the
car and as a beneficial sports practice for health.

3

Hour record.

Beating the hour record is the great achievement sought by many cyclists since Henri Desgrange set the first mark at 35.325 km in 1893.

Legend Eddy Merckx, in 1972, raised the mark to 49.431 km.

Only the Spaniard Miguel Indurain, in 1994, managed to inscribe Spain's name in such a notable book, with 53.040 km.

Currently, Belgian Victor Campenaerts holds the record with 55.089 km, achieved in 2019.

4

Increase mobility by bike.

The use of bicycles in big cities is
increasing more and more.

This means of transportation has replaced
cars or motorcycles for daily commutes.

Nearly 90% of the Spanish population knows how
to ride a bike, as we can see from the
data of the Bicycle Barometer 2019.

More than 21 million Spaniards have
bicycles for personal use.

Barcelona is the city with the most bikes in Europe,
only surpassed by Amsterdam.

It is estimated that there are approximately
one billion bicycles worldwide.

The number of bicycles would double that of cars.

In China, for example, there are about 450 million
bicycles, and for every car, there are 250 bicycles.

5

The 19 monuments of Merckx.

Since the taste of victory in his first
Milan-San Remo, at just 20 years
old, Eddy Merckx's performance
has been unbeatable in the
spring cycling classics.

He accumulated more wins than any
other cyclist, including 5 of the
classics with the greatest history in
the international cycling calendar,
known as the Monuments of Cycling.

These are: 7 Milan-San Remo, 5
Liege-Bastogne-Liege, 2 Tour
of Flanders, 3 Paris-Roubaix,
and 2 Tour of Lombardy.

6

Cycling and sexual function.

Many false myths have arisen regarding the relationship between cycling activity and erectile dysfunction, leading to different studies by the American Urological Society.

The studies conclude that cycling does not worsen urinary symptoms or erectile function.

Instead, it is observed that cycling improves sexual arousal and satisfaction levels.

7

Caloric expenditure of the cyclist.

The intensity of effort required to cover a race is only compensated by the consumption of large caloric portions.

A cyclist may require up to twice the calories that a footballer consumes, i.e., a minimum of 6,000 calories per day.

This is equivalent to more than 50 protein shakes or 12 Big Macs.

As preparation for covering the cycling classics, caloric consumption can even double.

8

**The brands B.H., Orbea, and G.A.C. are well-known for their
presence in the bicycle industry, but they also have
an interesting history behind them.**

These brands emerged in the early 20th century and their main
activity at that time was the manufacturing of weapons.

However, as the demand for weapons decreased, these
companies saw an opportunity in bicycle manufacturing.

They started producing high-quality bicycles and gradually
specialized completely in bicycle production.

B.H. is a Spanish brand founded in 1909 that specializes in the
production of road bikes, electric bikes, and mountain bikes.

Its name comes from Beistegui Hermanos,
the company's founders.

Orbea, another Spanish brand, was founded in 1840
and began producing bicycles in 1930.

Today, it is one of the most recognized brands in the cycling
world and specializes in road bikes, mountain bikes,
urban bikes, and electric bikes.

Lastly, G.A.C. is a Spanish brand founded in 1901.

In its early years, it was dedicated to the production of weapons
and agricultural machinery, but later specialized
in bicycle production.

It is currently known for its urban and leisure bikes.

9

Tour de France.

The Tour de France was created on January 1, 1903, and in the early editions, stages of over 400 kilometers were disputed at night, on dusty roads full of hardships, something incredibly tough, even for today's professional cyclists.

Additionally, it is the third most covered sports event in the world, surpassed only by the World Cup and the Olympics.

10

Giro d'Italia's Pink Jersey.

Also called the maglia rosa, it was in 1931 when the leader of the race was first dressed in this color to easily distinguish him from the rest of the peloton.

The reason for choosing this color was in honor of the Gazzetta dello Sport, the main organizer of the race that at that time used this tone to characterize its pages.

11

Julien Absalon is one of the most successful and recognized mountain bikers in the world.

Born in France in 1980, Absalon started his mountain biking career at the age of 16 and quickly stood out as one of the most promising talents in the cross-country discipline.

During his career, Absalon won an impressive number of titles and medals around the world.

Among his most notable achievements are his two Olympic gold medals, obtained in Athens 2004 and Beijing 2008 in the cross-country category.

In addition, Absalon also won five cross-country world championships, four UCI Mountain Bike World Cup titles, and multiple national and continental championships.

In total, he accumulated more than 30 victories in the UCI Mountain Bike World Cup, becoming the cyclist with the most victories in the history of the discipline.

Absalon is considered by many as the "king of MTB" due to his dominance in the cross-country discipline for much of his career.

His aggressive riding style and technical ability on difficult terrains made him an impressive and feared cyclist by his rivals.

In the later years of his career, Absalon retired from the cross-country discipline to focus on enduro races, where he also had success and won several races.

Throughout his career, he stood out for his dedication and commitment to the sport, earning him the respect and admiration of many MTB cyclists and fans around the world.

12

**Federico Martin Bahamontes, also known as the
"Eagle of Toledo," is a legend of Spanish cycling.**

Born in 1928 in Toledo, Bahamontes started his professional
cycling career in 1954 and soon became one of the most
successful and popular riders of his time.

One of the highlights of his career was his victory in the 1959 Tour
de France, becoming the first Spaniard to win this prestigious race.

He also won the King of the Mountains jersey in the Tour de France
six times and won several stages in important races such as the
Vuelta a España, the Giro d'Italia, and the Paris-Nice.

Bahamontes was known for his ability in the mountains,
which earned him the nickname "Eagle of Toledo."

In addition, his charismatic personality and risky style
on the bike made him a favorite among fans.

Before becoming a professional cyclist, Bahamontes was involved
in smuggling, an illegal activity that involved trading
products outside of legal distribution channels.

Cycling offered him an opportunity to get out of this
situation and become a successful athlete.

After retiring from professional cycling in 1965, Bahamontes
dedicated himself to training young cyclists and also
became a cycling commentator for Spanish television.

In recognition of his career, he was named "Best Spanish Cyclist
of the 20th Century" by the Spanish Cycling Federation in 1999.

13

Cycling and well-being.

A study published in the Journal of Diabetes Complications showed that after 12 weeks of cycling, participants in the study gained much more than leg strength.

The brain activity of these individuals increased, which led to an increase in a brain neurotrophic factor, producing an increase in a protein responsible for regulating stress, mood, and memory.

This justifies another theory that links cycling practice with lower levels of depression and anxiety.

14

Michael Secrest is an American cyclist who excelled in the discipline of ultra-distance.

In 1990, he set the world record for the distance covered on a bicycle in a 24-hour period.

At that time, Secrest managed to cover an impressive distance of 1958 kilometers in a single day, thus surpassing the previous record set by another American cyclist, John Howard.

This achievement is considered one of the greatest in the history of ultra-distance cycling.

To achieve this record, Secrest had to maintain an average speed of more than 80 km/h for 24 hours straight, without stopping to rest.

To do so, he prepared intensively for months, focusing on his physical and mental training, as well as the strategy he had to follow during the race.

Secrest's record remains the world record for the distance covered on a bicycle in a 24-hour period.

Since then, other cyclists have attempted to surpass it, but no one has managed to beat the mark established by Secrest in 1990.

15

The Spanish cyclist who doped with cod.

One of the first Spaniards to participate in the Tour de France was Vicente Blanco, who, after losing his left foot and the toes on his right foot in two different work accidents, decided to participate in the Tour.

Very few people actually believed that Blanco could finish the race, but he, trying to prove his bravery, also said that he would do it without eating.

Although this is what Vicente Blanco told the organizers and other participants, what really happened is that his friends hid food for him at strategic points along the route.

This is how, in a somewhat special way, he became the cyclist who first used doping.

16

René Vietto was a French cyclist who competed in the 1930s and 1940s.

During his career, Vietto achieved several victories in major races such as the Tour de France, the Vuelta a Francia, and the Milan-San Remo.

In 1934, while competing in the Tour de France, Vietto was about to win a stage on his own when he came across his team leader, Antonin Magne, who had suffered a breakdown on his bicycle.

Despite being only a few kilometers from the finish line, Vietto decided to turn back and climb the mountain he had just descended to find Magne and give him his own bicycle, allowing him to continue the race.

This action was a great gesture of camaraderie and loyalty from Vietto, who sacrificed his own victory in the stage to help his teammate.

Although he did not win the stage, Vietto earned the respect and admiration of cycling fans around the world.

Vietto continued to compete in the Tour de France in the following years, achieving several stage victories and being a prominent rider in the general classifications.

After retiring from professional cycling in the 1940s, he became a successful coach and sports director, helping to train some of the best French cyclists of the time.

17

**France is the country with the most victories
in the history of the Tour de France,
with a total of 36 victories.**

However, it is also true that no French cyclist has won
the race since Bernard Hinault's victory in 1985, which
has led many to talk about the "curse of the Tour
de France" for French riders.

Since Hinault's victory, several French cyclists have
come close to winning the Tour de France, such
as Laurent Fignon, Jean-Francois Bernard, and
Richard Virenque, among others, but none
have been able to do so.

This "curse" has become a recurring theme in the
French press, and many experts have tried to explain
why French cyclists have not been able to
win the race in so many years.

Some of the theories that have been proposed include a
lack of investment in French teams, a lack of support
from sponsors, and the media pressure
surrounding French riders.

Despite everything, French fans continue to dream of the
day when a cyclist from their country will win the Tour
de France again, and every year they support French
riders in the hope that they can break the curse.

18

The most expensive bike in the world is called "The Beverly Hills Edition."

This bike was built from an aluminum frame coated with 24-carat gold, 600 black diamonds, and 500 sapphires embedded in its surface.

To ensure its comfort, the seat is covered in crocodile leather.

There are only 13 in the world, and its price is one million dollars.

There is also a bike made entirely of gold, with a price tag exceeding $100,000.

Its usefulness is doubtful, but it is undoubtedly beautiful.

19

Doping has been a problem in sports for a long time, and cycling has not been an exception.

In fact, some of the earliest doping cases in the history of sports occurred in cycling.

In the early years of cycling competitions, in the mid-19th and early 20th centuries, it was common for riders to consume substances like alcohol, caffeine, cocaine, and strychnine to try to improve their performance.

At that time, the use of these substances was not prohibited and was not considered cheating.

Over time, doping became more sophisticated, and increasingly dangerous and effective substances and methods were used to enhance performance.

The first doping substance to be banned in cycling was ephedrine in the 1960s, and since then, more and more substances have been added to the list of banned substances.

Despite efforts to combat doping in cycling and in sports in general, it remains a significant problem.

In cycling, many doping scandals have occurred in recent years, with cases like that of American Lance Armstrong and the Festina team, among others, seriously damaging the sport's image.

20

Gino Bartali is considered one of the great champions in the history of cycling and an anonymous hero during World War II.

During the war, Bartali collaborated with the Italian resistance and helped save the lives of hundreds of Jews.

Bartali used his fame and his skills as a cyclist to act as a messenger and deliver false documentation and other materials throughout Nazi-occupied Italy.

He would hide the documents and other items in the tube of his bicycle and often personally deliver them to their intended recipients.

This activity was very dangerous, as the Nazis were closely monitoring cyclists moving throughout the country.

In addition to helping the resistance and persecuted Jews, Bartali also used his influence and position to protect other people at risk, including friends and neighbors.

After the war, Bartali continued to compete in cycling and won three Tours de France, two Giri d'Italia, and a gold medal in the 1936 Olympics.

However, his role as an anonymous hero during the war is an important part of his legacy and a testament to his bravery and humanity in difficult times.

21

The "Draisine" was a revolutionary invention that laid the foundation for the creation of the modern bicycle.

It is also known as the "running machine" or "running device" and consisted of a two-wheeled vehicle with a handlebar and a saddle for the rider.

Unlike modern bicycles, it had no pedals, so the rider had to push themselves forward with their feet on the ground.

The "Draisine" was a great success in its time following its development in 1817 by German Karl Von Drais.

It allowed people to move faster and with less effort than walking, however, its use was limited due to the lack of suitable roads and paths for the transportation of this vehicle.

In the years following the invention of the "Draisine," different models of bicycles were developed that incorporated improvements and new functionalities, such as pedals, brakes, or chain transmission.

In this way, the bicycle became a popular and accessible means of transportation for people all over the world.

22

What is the difference between a men's and women's bike?

Women tend to have proportionally longer legs, a shorter torso, wider hips, shorter arms, and smaller hands and feet than men.

Frames are specifically designed for both women and men.

And the contact points have also been adapted to women's needs: narrower handlebars, shorter cranks, and wider, shorter saddles.

23

From 2015 to March 2023, there is no updated official record of the number of bicycles sold worldwide.

However, according to some reports from the bicycle industry, it is estimated that around 130 million bicycles were sold worldwide in 2020, largely driven by the increased demand for bicycles during the COVID-19 pandemic.

It is worth noting that the bicycle market is constantly growing and evolving, with an increasing trend towards electric bicycles and bicycles for urban and recreational use.

24

**A study by the University of Illinois
conducted a series of tests
on 12 fit cyclists.**

The study was based on giving some only
water, some energy gels, and others
mashed potatoes.

The results were very surprising because
those who consumed gels and mashed
potatoes obtained the same levels of
energy for prolonged physical exercise,
while those who only drank water did not.

However, to achieve the same glucose
levels as the gels, cyclists had to eat a lot
of mashed potatoes, so they experienced
some secondary problems.

25

Strava, the most popular sports app in the world, publishes an annual report with global trends based on the tens of millions of users on this social network.

In these studies, it has been found that since 2015, 67.9% of cyclists who registered cycling as their only sport has decreased to 47.2% in 2019, and has grown even more during the pandemic.

Among the other activities performed are hiking, yoga, and weight training.

26

In 2019, Shimano, one of the main manufacturers of components for bicycles, commissioned a survey from the company YouGov about the use of electric bicycles (e-bikes) in different countries around the world.

The survey involved 12,000 people from 10 countries, including Japan, the United States, the United Kingdom, Germany, France, Italy, the Netherlands, China, Australia, and Spain.

Among the survey results, it was found that 25% of respondents would be willing to ride an e-bike to work.

In Spain, the percentage was higher, with 39% of respondents willing to use an e-bike for commuting.

In addition, 72% of respondents said they would consider buying an e-bike at some point in the future, while the remaining 28% said they would not consider it.

Reasons for considering the purchase of an e-bike included the ease of climbing hills (54%), the possibility of reaching more distant destinations (49%), the reduction of travel time (46%), and the reduction of traffic congestion (41%).

27

What are the main health benefits of cycling?

-It helps improve the circulatory system.

-Burns body fat.

-Strengthens the immune system.

-Improves brain oxygenation.

-Increases muscle tone.

-Reduces the risk of serious illnesses.

-Improves lung function, helps prevent the onset of bone diseases.

-Lowers cholesterol and triglyceride levels.

-Helps regulate sleep.

-Reduces stress levels.

28

The bicycle has played an important role in the military of several countries throughout history.

In the case of France, its military use dates back to the late 19th century, when it began to be used for reconnaissance and as a means of transportation for troops.

In 1887, the world's first bicycle battalion was created, consisting of soldiers mounted on bicycles, who were used to patrol and carry out reconnaissance missions in difficult terrain.

Subsequently, other countries such as Germany and England also adopted the use of bicycles in the military, and bicycle battalions were created in other parts of the world such as the United States and Japan.

During World War I, the bicycle was used to transport supplies and personnel, and bicycles equipped with machine guns were also used for surprise attacks.

In World War II, the bicycle was once again used by the military, and specific models were developed for military tasks, such as the BSA folding bicycle, used by British forces for transportation by parachute and infiltration missions.

Currently, some military forces continue to use bicycles in their operations, especially for reconnaissance and patrolling in difficult terrain.

29

**The "Eta" bicycle is a model designed and built
by the Canadian team AeroVelo.**

It was specifically designed to set the world
record for bicycle speed.

In September 2015, on a special road built in Battle
Mountain, Nevada, rider Todd Reichert reached a speed of
139.45 km/h on the "Eta" bicycle, breaking the previous
record of 133.78 km/h set by the Dutch team VeloX in 2013.

The "Eta" bicycle uses a human-electric propulsion system
and has an extremely efficient aerodynamic design.

It is built with lightweight and strong materials,
such as carbon fiber and titanium, and has
a total weight of only 25 kg.

The rider is completely encapsulated in a fiberglass cabin
and lies in a nearly horizontal position to
minimize wind resistance.

The bicycle speed record is an annual event organized by the
International Human Powered Vehicle Association (IHPVA)
and attracts teams from around the world who
compete to establish the new world record.

AeroVelo's "Eta" bicycle has been the fastest
bicycle in the event since 2015.

30

Cycling around the world.

In 1884, Thomas Stevens became the first person to cycle around the world, a pioneer of bicycle travel and therefore of cycle tourism.

He started from San Francisco to Sacramento crossing the Sierra Nevada, Nevada, Utah, and Wyoming mountains.

He arrived in Boston after more than 5,000 kilometers through railroads, trails, and roads, to complete the first transcontinental journey.

Later, he planned his trip to Asia and for this, he relied on the help of an interpreter at the Chinese embassy who dissuaded him from cycling through Upper Burma and China, among other places.

His trip around the world ended after covering a distance of about 13,500 miles, or 21,700 kilometers.

After his adventure, he decided to collect all his experiences in a two-volume, 1,000-page book called "Around the World on a Bicycle."

31

The increase in bicycle use as a means of transportation can have important benefits for both the environment and health and the economy.

In the case of the United States, according to a report by the Institute for Transportation and Development Policy, increasing cycling from 1% to 1.5% of all trips could save 1.748.86 billion liters of gasoline per year.

In the case of Tokyo, a city with significant traffic and congestion problems, it has been shown that in most trips of less than 50 minutes, a bicycle is faster than a car.

In addition, 20 bicycles can be parked in the same space occupied by a car, making the bicycle a much more efficient option in terms of space and use of urban land.

Overall, the use of bicycles as a means of transportation can contribute to reducing traffic congestion, improving air quality, promoting a healthier lifestyle, and reducing dependence on fossil fuels.

Therefore, promoting and encouraging the use of bicycles is one of the most important strategies for achieving more sustainable and livable cities.

32

A bicycle can be composed of hundreds of parts, and the exact number may vary depending on the model and brand.

In addition to the chain, some of the most important parts of a bicycle include the frame, fork, handlebars, wheels, tires, brakes, gears, saddle, and bottom bracket.

The frame is the main structure of the bicycle and can be made of different materials such as steel, aluminum, carbon, or titanium.

The fork is the part that holds the front wheel and is usually made of the same material as the frame.

The handlebars are the part that the cyclist grips to control the direction and can have different shapes and materials depending on the intended use of the bicycle.

The wheels are usually composed of the rim, spokes, and hub, which is the central part where the wheel is attached to the frame.

The tires are the part that comes into contact with the ground and can vary in size and shape depending on the type of bicycle.

The brakes can be of different types, such as rim brakes, hydraulic disc brakes, or drum brakes.

The gear system allows the cyclist to change the ratio between the chainring (the part where the bottom bracket is fixed) and the cassette (the part that rotates with the rear wheel), which allows for greater efficiency on different terrains and situations.

The saddle is the part where the cyclist sits and can vary in size and shape depending on personal preferences and the intended use of the bicycle.

The bottom bracket is the part where the pedals are fixed and usually includes the crankset.

33

10 countries with the highest percentage of bicycle use in the world:

1.Netherlands: with an impressive 99% ratio, it is the country where bicycles are most commonly used. The Dutch government has invested in appropriate cycling infrastructure, including bicycle lanes, bicycle parking, and a network of bicycle routes connecting cities.

2.Denmark: is known for being bicycle-friendly, with 80% of the population using bicycles as a mode of transportation. Danish cities are designed for cycling, with bicycle lanes separated from main roads and special traffic lights for bicycles.

3.Germany: with a 76% ratio, the German government has invested in bicycle infrastructure and promoted the use of electric bicycles, which are a popular option for longer trips.

4.Sweden: 64% of the population uses bicycles as a mode of transportation. Like Denmark, Sweden has separated bicycle lanes and special traffic lights for bicycles.

5.Norway: with a ratio of 60.6%, it has seen an increase in bicycle use in recent years. Bicycles are a popular option in both cities and rural areas, with well-developed bicycle lanes and routes.

6.Finland: with a ratio of 60.4%, the Finnish government has invested in bicycle infrastructure, including bicycle lanes and routes connecting cities.

7.Japan: has a ratio of 56.9%, bicycles are popular in Japanese cities, with bicycle lanes and bicycle parking at major train stations.

8.Switzerland: with a ratio of 49.4%, Swiss cities have well-developed bicycle lanes and there are numerous bicycle routes throughout the country.

9.Belgium: with a ratio of 48%, Belgian cities have bicycle lanes and special traffic lights for bicycles, and the bicycle is a popular option for daily commutes.

10.China: with a ratio of 37.2%, it is the most populous country in the world and, although car usage has been increasing in recent years, the bicycle remains a very popular mode of transportation in Chinese cities, especially for short trips.

34

Average salary of the riders in the top 2 categories of cycling:

-ProTeam Cyclist. This is the category below WorldTour, so it would be a second division. The minimum salary for a rider is approximately €32,000 per year. This would be the minimum amount that a rider in the ProTour category would earn, according to Zikloland magazine. A salary that allows them to live comfortably, without the need for another job. We could say that the cyclists competing in this category can earn a decent living. Depending on each rider's contract, the remuneration varies.

-WorldTour Cyclists. This would be the first division of cycling, where the best teams and riders from around the world are, and obviously, the highest salaries. Within this category, the minimum salary a rider would earn is approximately €40,000 per year, a significant improvement compared to the salary of ProTeam cyclists. Within this category, you can find the best cyclists in the world, and obviously, their salaries have nothing to do with those of other cyclists in the peloton. In the WorldTour category, you can find highly recognized teams such as the Movistar Team, Team Ineos, Astana, or Bora-Hansgrohe, among others.

35

**Vincenzo Nibali is an Italian cyclist
born in Messina in 1984.**

He has been one of the most successful cyclists of the
last decade, with victories in the three major tours: the
Giro d'Italia, the Tour de France, and the Vuelta a España.

In addition to these achievements, Nibali has also won
important classics such as Liege-Bastogne-Liege
and the Tour of Lombardy.

Regarding his salary, until 2019 he was among the
highest-paid cyclists in the international peloton with
nearly €4 million, but his move to the Trek Segafredo
team and his more modest results in recent years have
led to a salary reduction to €2.1 million in 2021.

After his move to the Astana team in 2022, it is
estimated that his salary could be even lower.

In the 2016 Giro d'Italia, Nibali demonstrated his great
quality by winning the race in a spectacular way,
surpassing his rivals in a stage where he had to climb
the fearsome mountain pass of Passo dello Stelvio,
with snow and sub-zero temperatures.

This triumph made him one of the few cyclists in
history to win the three major tours and
earned him the nickname "The Shark".

36

Alejandro Valverde was born on April 25, 1980 in Murcia, Spain, and began his professional cycling career in 2002 with the Kelme-Costa Blanca team.

Since then, he has competed for some of the biggest teams in the cycling world, including Caisse d'Epargne and the current Movistar Team.

Valverde has won major cycling races around the world, including the 2009 Vuelta a España, the 2006, 2008, 2015, and 2017 Liège-Bastogne-Liège, and the 2006, 2014, and 2015 Fleche Wallonne.

He has also achieved multiple victories in other important races, such as the Clásica de San Sebastián and the Vuelta al País Vasco.

Furthermore, in 2018, Valverde became the Road Cycling World Champion, winning the World Championship that year in Innsbruck, Austria.

This victory was very significant for him and for Spanish cycling, as it was the first time a Spanish cyclist had won the World Championship in over a decade.

Valverde has also been the subject of controversy in his career.

In 2010, he was suspended for two years due to his involvement in the Operación Puerto, a doping network in Spain.

However, despite this suspension, he has managed to stay at the top of the cycling world and remain a highly respected cyclist.

As for his salary, Valverde is estimated to earn around 2.2 million euros per year, making him one of the highest-paid cyclists in the peloton.

In 2022, he announced that it would be his last season as a professional cyclist, closing a career full of successes and remarkable achievements in the world of cycling.

37

Julian Alaphilippe is a French professional cyclist who currently competes for the Deceuninck-QuickStep team.

He was born on June 11, 1992 in Saint-Amand-Montrond, France.

He began his cycling career in 2013 with the amateur team Armée de Terre, before joining the WorldTour team Etixx-QuickStep in 2014.

Alaphilippe is known for his ability in one-day races, especially in spring classics such as the Fleche Wallonne and Strade Bianche.

He is also a strong rider in stage races and has won several stages in the world's most important stage race, the Tour de France.

In 2019, Alaphilippe caused a big surprise by leading the Tour de France for 14 days and winning two stages, before finishing fifth in the overall classification.

He has also won other major races such as Milan-San Remo and the Clásica de San Sebastián.

In 2020, Alaphilippe won the Road Cycling World Championship in Imola, Italy, becoming the first Frenchman to win the title in 23 years.

He repeated the feat in 2021 in Flanders, Belgium, making him the first cyclist to win the world title twice in a row since Paolo Bettini in 2006 and 2007.

As for his salary, it is estimated that Alaphilippe earned 2.3 million euros in 2021, making him one of the highest-paid cyclists in the peloton.

This salary increase came after winning the 2020 World Championship and repeating the feat in 2021.

38

Michal Kwiatkowski is a Polish professional cyclist born in 1990.

He began his career with the Spanish Continental team Caja Rural in 2010 and then moved to the WorldTour team Omega Pharma-Quick Step in 2013.

In 2014, Kwiatkowski had a successful season, winning several major races, including the Amstel Gold Race and the Clásica San Sebastián, and also won the World Championship in Ponferrada, Spain.

In 2016, Kwiatkowski joined Team Sky (now known as INEOS Grenadiers) and has been an important support rider for team leaders in races such as the Tour de France.

He has also achieved some important victories, such as the Strade Bianche in 2017 and 2021.

Kwiatkowski's salary in 2021 was 2.5 million euros, making him one of the highest-paid cyclists in the peloton.

However, his salary has also been criticized by some in the cycling community due to the tendency of WorldTour teams to pay high salaries to a few star riders, while lower-ranked cyclists receive much lower salaries.

39

Egan Bernal is a Colombian professional cyclist born on January 13, 1997 in Zipaquirá, Colombia.

He began cycling at the age of 8 and at 16 moved to Italy to further his cycling career.

In 2016, Bernal was selected by the Androni Giocattoli-Sidermec team for his professional debut in cycling.

That same year, he won the Tour de l'Avenir, an important cycling race for under-23 cyclists, and was signed by the Italian WorldTour team, Team Sky (now known as INEOS Grenadiers).

In 2019, Bernal was one of the leaders of the Ineos team in the Tour de France and managed to win the race, becoming the first Colombian cyclist to do so.

In 2020, he suffered a back injury that forced him to withdraw from the Tour de France, but he returned to compete in 2021 and won the Tour de Suisse.

Bernal is considered one of the best climbers in the peloton, and his aggressive and courageous cycling style has won admiration around the world.

His salary on the Ineos team is estimated at 2.8 million euros, placing him among the highest-paid cyclists in the peloton.

40

Geraint Thomas is a British cyclist born on May 25, 1986 in Cardiff, Wales.

He began his professional career in 2007 with the Barloworld team and since then has achieved numerous victories and important accomplishments in his career.

Specialized in stage races, he won the Tour de France in 2018, in addition to other important titles such as Paris-Nice, Critérium du Dauphiné, and Volta ao Algarve.

Since 2010, he has been a member of the Sky/Ineos Grenadiers team, one of the most powerful teams in the peloton, where he has played both the role of support rider and team leader in different races.

His salary of 3.5 million euros places him among the highest-paid cyclists in the peloton and reflects his ability to lead a team in important races.

41

**Thomas Pidcock is a British cyclist
born in Leeds in 1999.**

He started in mountain biking and road cycling
at a young age and quickly stood out for
his skills in both disciplines.

In 2021, he won the gold medal in the cross-
country race at the Tokyo Olympics and also won
the Cyclocross World Championship in 2022.

Currently, Pidcock rides for the Ineos Grenadiers
team, one of the most important teams in the
international peloton, and his contract has
been extended until 2027 with a salary of
4 million euros per season.

At 23 years old, he is considered one of the most
promising cyclists in the world, capable of
competing both in the mountains and
on the road and in cyclocross.

In addition to his victories in MTB and cyclocross,
he has also achieved podiums and victories in
prestigious road races, such as the Tour de
l'Avenir and the Paris-Roubaix Sub-23.

42

Chris Froome is a British cyclist born in Kenya.

He is one of the most successful cyclists in the history of road cycling, having won the Tour de France four times in his career, as well as the Vuelta a España twice and the Giro d'Italia once.

However, in recent years he has suffered several setbacks, including a serious crash in 2019 that left him with multiple injuries and kept him away from competition for several months.

In 2021, Froome joined the Israel Start-Up Nation team, where he is estimated to earn an annual salary of 5 million euros, making him one of the highest-paid cyclists in the peloton.

Although he has had some notable performances in the races he has participated in, he has not yet fully recovered his old form and has faced some criticism for his performance.

43

Peter Sagan is a Slovak cyclist born on January 26, 1990.

He is considered one of the best cyclists of his generation, known for his great versatility on different terrains and sprinting abilities.

Sagan began his professional career with the Liquigas-Doimo team in 2010 and has since accumulated numerous victories and important titles.

Among his achievements are three consecutive titles in the UCI Road World Championships (2015, 2016, and 2017), seven stages of the Tour de France, five of the Giro d'Italia, and seventeen in the Vuelta a España.

He has also won important classics such as Paris-Roubaix, Gent-Wevelgem, and Strade Bianche.

In terms of his salary, it is estimated to be between 5 and 5.5 million euros annually, which puts him among the highest-paid cyclists in the peloton.

A significant part of this salary is contributed by Specialized, his main sponsor, who has designed customized bicycles for him and created a line of products under his name.

Sagan also has a large following on social media, leading the ranking of cyclists with the most followers.

44

**Tadej Pogacar is a Slovenian professional cyclist
born on September 21, 1998.**

He began his career with the Ljubljana Gusto Santic team in 2016,
before joining the Slovenian Roglic team in 2018.

In 2019, he joined the UAE Emirates team and quickly showed
his talent by winning the general classification of the
Tour of California and the Tour de l'Avenir.

In 2020, Pogacar achieved his greatest success by winning the
Tour de France, becoming the second youngest cyclist
to win the race after Henri Cornet in 1904.

In addition to the general classification, he also won
three stages and the mountain classification.

In 2021, he successfully defended his title in the
Tour de France, winning two stages along the way.

After his success in the 2020 Tour de France, Pogacar renewed
his contract with the UAE Emirates team until 2024.

However, after his victory in the 2021 Tour de France, the team
announced that they had extended his contract until 2027
and that his salary had increased to 6 million euros annually,
making him one of the highest-paid cyclists in the world.

Pogacar has also won several other important races, such as
the Vuelta a España and Liège-Bastogne-Liège, and is
considered one of the best cyclists of his generation.

Despite his youth, he has already shown to be a complete
rider capable of winning races of all types and terrains,
and many see him as the future of cycling.

45

Jennie Longo is a legend of French women's cycling, born in Annecy in 1958.

She started her career in track cycling, winning several medals in French and international championships.

She later focused on road cycling, where she achieved most of her accomplishments.

Throughout her career, Jennie Longo won a total of 59 national championships and 13 world championships in different disciplines, including track and road cycling, as well as individual time trial.

She also won three Olympic medals, two silver and one bronze, and was the first cyclist to win the Tour de l'Aude four times.

Longo was known for her ability to compete at the highest level for many seasons, even after becoming a mother in 1987.

She continued to compete in international-level championships until the age of 53, when she decided to retire in 2012.

Her legacy in women's cycling is undeniable and has been an inspiration for many cyclists who have come after her.

46

Fabian Cancellara is a retired Swiss cyclist who retired in 2016.

He is considered one of the greatest time trial cyclists in history, having won 4 time trial world championships in 2006, 2007, 2009, and 2010.

He has also won two Olympic gold medals in individual time trial at Beijing 2008 and London 2012.

Additionally, he has won several important classics such as Paris-Roubaix and Tour of Flanders multiple times.

Cancellara is known for his powerful and aerodynamic pedaling style and his ability to take corners at high speeds.

He is also nicknamed "Spartacus" for his strength and endurance.

47

Being able to wear the rainbow colors on the jersey is one of the greatest honors a professional cyclist can receive, as it represents being the world champion in a specific discipline (road, time trial, track, etc.).

The design of the rainbow jersey consists of horizontal stripes of the colors of the rainbow: red, orange, yellow, green, blue, indigo, and violet, which represent the diversity and unity of international cycling.

Additionally, the world champion cyclist has the right to keep the rainbow colors on their jersey throughout the rest of their sports career, although they can only wear it in the discipline in which they won the title.

If a cyclist wins the world championship in several disciplines, as may be the case for track cyclists who compete in different events, they can wear the rainbow colors on the jerseys of each of those disciplines.

It is important to mention that, although the rainbow jersey is a great honor for the cyclist who wears it, the leader's jersey of any race takes precedence over the world champion's jersey, so the race leader may not wear the rainbow colors if another cyclist with a world champion's jersey is also participating in the race.

48

Mikkel Bjerg is a Danish cyclist born on February 3, 1998.

He is known for his success in the under-23 time trial discipline, in which he has won the World Championship three times.

His first victory in the under-23 Time Trial World Championship was in 2017, in Bergen, Norway, where he beat his compatriot Mathias Norsgaard Jørgensen and Russian Aleksandr Vlasov.

Bjerg set a time of 32:39, at an average speed of 49.347 km/h.

In 2018, Bjerg repeated the feat in Innsbruck, Austria, where he again defeated Norsgaard Jørgensen and Belgian Brent Van Moer, setting a time of 33:01, at an average speed of 48.548 km/h.

In 2019, Bjerg achieved his third consecutive title in the under-23 Time Trial World Championship in Yorkshire, England.

On this occasion, he beat Swiss Stefan Bissegger and Dutch Daan Hoole, setting a time of 38:28, at an average speed of 50.164 km/h.

In addition to his successes in the under-23 Time Trial World Championship, Bjerg has also excelled in other competitions.

In 2018, he won the National Time Trial Championship in Denmark, and in 2019 he won the silver medal in the individual time trial at the European Games in Minsk.

Regarding his professional career, Bjerg has ridden for the Danish team ColoQuick since 2017.

In 2021, he made the jump to the WorldTour by signing with the UAE Team Emirates, where he has ridden alongside renowned cyclists such as Tadej Pogacar and Matteo Trentin.

49

The revolution of developments.

In the last few decades, cycling materials have undergone a significant evolution, starting with bicycles that are increasingly lighter and stiffer, and continuing with the rest of the components: clothing, accessories, etc.

The appearance of modern cyclists is far from what they looked like a couple of decades ago.

The development of a bicycle, meaning the combination and size of chainrings and cogs, has undergone a spectacular change in just a decade.

The variety of possible gear ratios today is infinitely greater than what even professional road cyclists in the 1980s or early 1990s could use.

For starters, we have gone from having only 2x6 or 2x7 gear options to 2x11, which can be found in almost any medium or high-end bicycle model.

But perhaps more important than the number of gear options is the appearance of the so-called "compact" gear ratios about a decade ago.

50

Clipless pedals.

The 1985 Tour was won by Frenchman Bernard Hinault.

It was his fifth and last triumphant Tour, and he did it by almost single-handedly embracing a technological advancement in the cycling revolution: clipless pedals.

Hinault had always gotten along well with technical innovations (his La Vie Claire team was the first to bet on bikes with carbon tubes).

The idea for clipless pedals came from alpine skiing, a sport that had been using such bindings for securing skis to feet for years and that could release automatically when necessary.

Hinault would participate in another Tour, the 1986 edition, almost exclusively using these automatic bindings.

Interestingly, many great cyclists found it difficult to give up the classic pedals with toe clips: Stephen Roche even won the 1987 Tour with traditional pedals, Lucho Herrera also rode the peaks that way... and Miguel Indurain was one of the last to abandon the traditional pedals; not a big fan of innovations, the Spanish champion was still using them in 1989, when clipless pedals had already become widespread in the cycling revolution.

51

Gear shifters integrated into the brake levers.

Another classic image of cycling in the 70s and 80s was seeing cyclists reaching down to the frame to shift gears.

It's important to remember that, at that time, the small levers were not indexed or synchronized, so shifting between the chainrings and cassette was done "by feel".

This, as you can imagine, caused a lot of problems and more than one racer lost a race due to not being in the right gear.

In fact, choosing the right gear was crucial in sprint finishes, as once the "sprint" was launched, it was impossible to shift.

Shimano was the first components brand to introduce integrated shifters into the brake levers around 1985.

It's worth noting that the technical advance in the bike revolution here was twofold: putting the shifters on the handlebars, and, very importantly, making them indexed: one click now equaled one gear shift.

Nevertheless, in those years Shimano was not the giant that now dominates the cycling market.

The rest of the brands (Campagnolo, Suntour, Mavic, etc.) took a few more years to adopt integrated shifters as a new standard.

Interestingly, Miguel Indurain was the first cyclist to win the Tour de France on a bike equipped with shifters on the brake levers; he did it on his white Pinarello in 1992.

52

Evolution of gear ratios.

Perico Delgado has explained more than once that he won his 1988 Tour de France with a maximum gear ratio of 42x25 (seven cogs).

In the 90s, the small chainring of 39 teeth became common, but it wasn't until well into the 21st century (2005-2006) that the so-called "compact" gear ratios, installed on 10-speed shifters, became popular.

This coincided with the boom in cycling during the bike revolution.

Cycling, both on the road and off-road, was becoming more popular, and this forced manufacturers to offer more affordable gear ratios for a less prepared type of enthusiast.

The compact ratios involved a combination of chainrings of 50/34 and a cassette with a range of 11-25; this allowed less experienced users to climb with some ease.

But spurred on by unprecedented sales success and customer demand, the industry made efforts to go further, and from 2010, 11-speed groups started to appear, offering cassettes with a range of 11-32 (this is a simplification as currently possible combinations allow for 12-speed groups with large chainrings up to 34 teeth, semi-compact chainrings of 52/36, and even single-chainring groups with up to 13 cogs).

53

Reimund Dietzen: Coteflabo accident.

That accident ended the career of German cyclist Reimund Dietzen and forced a change in regulations by the UCI.

On May 6, 1989, the 12th stage of the Vuelta a España was held under favorable weather conditions, between Benasque and Jaca (161 km).

At that time, the Spanish race was the first of the three Grand Tours and was held between late April and early May.

On that day's route, the cyclists climbed the Cotefablo pass from Biescas, which has an almost 700m long tunnel at its peak.

That tunnel is now illuminated, but it wasn't back then.

The reports of the time state that Unipublic, the organizer of the Vuelta, had commissioned a third party to illuminate the tunnel.

However, when the advance motorcycles of the Civil Guard arrived there, the tunnel was completely dark.

Some say that the police used their motorcycles to light the way for the cyclists, while others say that the race organizers asked them to advance to clear the way for the cyclists inside the tunnel.

54

The tragedy was foreseeable.

Cycling through a 700m tunnel in complete darkness (beyond the few lights and glow of the cars and motorcycles accompanying the peloton) was a dangerous situation.

The crash occurred in the middle of the peloton and fully caught German cyclist Reimund Dietzen.

Helmets were also not used at that time, and the blow to the head was strong: a skull fracture.

Although he tried, Reimund Dietzen never returned to professional cycling, and he retired at the end of the season.

The consequences of that head injury prevented him from continuing in the peloton.

7 years later, the race insurer was forced to compensate him with 80 million pesetas (now 48,000 €).

55

Bicycle transmissions:
2x10, 11, 12 speeds...

Do we need so many gears for road bikes?

Just over 15 years ago, road bikes had 9 speeds (and two chainrings, obviously).

In recent years, technological development, marketing, and the expansion of cycling as a leisure sport have driven an innovation that many consider excessive in cycling components...

Some say that going from 9 to 11 speeds in road groupsets is a real advance, but beyond this, especially if we use two chainrings, it doesn't make much sense simply because the gear ratios overlap with each other.

56

Monsieur Eugène Christophe's Forge.

In the early editions of the race, participants were only allowed to use a single bicycle for the entire event, which made cyclists responsible for repairing their bicycles in case of a breakdown.

At that time, Eugène Christophe had already proven himself in the grueling French tour, was one of the top favorites, and seemed poised to finally conquer the "big loop" that year.

Halfway through the race, he had already won three stages, including the feat of achieving victory with the most kilometers covered solo: 315 kilometers.

About 10 kilometers from the end of the descent, his bicycle fork broke.

His rivals began to overtake him.

Remember that mechanical assistance is prohibited.

There are no team cars, neutral cars, or helpers to assist.

The Tour de France is a solo adventure and Eugène Christophe was about to experience what that rule really meant...

First, he had to walk those 10 kilometers downhill, pushing his broken bike with the fork.

Upon reaching Sante Marie de Campan, he looked for the town's blacksmith, Mr. Lecomte, and asked for help in repairing his bike.

When they were about to start, one of the race commissioners arrived and warned him that no one could repair the bike for the rider, and that it had to be Christophe himself who had to do it personally.

So the cyclist got to work following the blacksmith's instructions and with the help of Corni, a seven-year-old boy who operated the bellows of the forge.

It took Christophe three hours to repair his bicycle.

In addition, Corni's help resulted in an extra 3-minute penalty.

The cyclist filled his pockets with bread and set off, heading towards the start of the Aspin pass.

He would eventually finish 7th overall in the 1913 Tour.

57

Raymond Poulidor was a French cyclist born on April 15, 1936 in Masbaraud-Mérignat, France.

Poulidor is known as the "eternal second" because he never won the Tour de France, despite trying 14 times and achieving second place three times and third place five times.

Poulidor made his debut in the Tour de France in 1962, and achieved his first podium finish in 1964 when he finished in second place behind Jacques Anquetil.

Poulidor and Anquetil maintained a great rivalry throughout their careers, and on several occasions they faced each other on the road for the victory in the Tour de France.

In 1966, Poulidor again finished in second place behind Anquetil, who achieved his fourth Tour title.

After Anquetil's retirement, Belgian Eddy Merckx became the new dominant force in cycling in the 1970s, and Poulidor continued to compete alongside him.

In 1974, Poulidor finished in third place in the Tour de France behind Merckx and Frenchman Vicente López Carril.

Poulidor also excelled in other races, winning the Vuelta a España in 1964, the Paris-Nice in 1972, and the Fleche Wallonne in 1963 and 1970.

In total, he achieved more than 180 victories throughout his career.

Poulidor was one of the most beloved cyclists in France and became a symbol for the working and rural class.

He worked as a farmer before becoming a professional cyclist and always maintained his humble rural roots.

After retiring from cycling in 1977, Poulidor worked as a sports commentator for French television.

He died on November 13, 2019, at the age of 83.

58

The frame and the fork are two of the most important components of a modern bicycle.

The frame is the structure that joins all the parts of the bicycle, including the handlebar, fork, and wheels.

It is designed to support most of the weight and resist the tension and forces generated by pedaling and uneven terrain.

The fork is the component that connects the front wheel to the frame.

It is designed to absorb vibrations and impacts from the terrain and provide stable and precise steering.

The fork is composed of two tubes that join at the base and attach to the head tube of the frame.

At the top of the fork is the steerer tube, which holds the handlebar and allows the cyclist to steer the bike.

Before the invention of the "safety" bicycle in the late 19th century, the most common bicycle was the Penny-Farthing, also known as the high-wheeler bicycle.

The Penny-Farthing had a huge front wheel and a small rear wheel, which made the bicycle very unstable and dangerous to ride.

The invention of the "safety" bicycle was a major breakthrough in cycling safety and comfort, as it allowed people to ride bicycles without the risk of serious falls and injuries.

Since then, bicycle frames and forks have been continuously developed and improved to offer better performance, safety, and comfort for cyclists around the world.

59

Rubber tires.

It was an essential contribution to the late
19th century bicycle boom, which we
owe to John Dunlop.

The use of a vulcanized rubber tire with an
inner air tube made bicycles viable and truly
suitable for riding for hours on paths
and the incipient roads of the time.

Until then, people rode directly
on iron or wooden wheels.

Michelin later perfected Dunlop's invention
by manufacturing the more commercial
and efficient disposable tire.

This invention was so important that it
marked the definitive takeoff of cycling as
a professional sport, with the emergence
of the first major classics such
as Liege and Roubaix.

60

The lightness of materials.

The first racing bicycles were made of iron or steel and probably weighed around 20 kg.

The great revolution in this regard was due to the introduction of carbon in the mass production of bicycles.

A plastic element that allows for rigid, comfortable, durable, and very lightweight structures.

A material that also does not rust and can be molded almost without limits.

It was with the proliferation of carbon bicycles in the early 21st century that the UCI decided to establish a minimum weight limit of 6.8 kg.

However, the industry is known to be able to offer durable bikes well below 6 kg.

61

Gear ratios.

It's curious, but the rear derailleurs in the evolution of bicycles, although invented a few years earlier, were not introduced in the Tour de France until 1937.

Why?

Simply because they were not allowed.

The only thing that was accepted by the regulations was that the wheels had two sprockets, one on each side of the rear wheel.

On climbs, riders had to dismount and turn the wheel to change gear ratios.

By the time the TDF allowed gear changes on bikes, they were already cable-operated with parallelogram derailleur.

There were earlier, more rudimentary gear changes that used levers to change the chain from one sprocket to another.

However, the great revolution in this area was the introduction, by Shimano, of indexed cable gear changes, in which each click of the lever corresponded to a movement of the chain.

In the mid-90s, Shimano also popularized integrated gear changes in the brake levers (until then, they were on the frame's top tube).

62

Triathlon handlebars.

Without a doubt, the latest great innovation in the world and evolution of the bike.

Used in triathlons a couple of years earlier, the boom of this accessory was in the 1989 TDF with Greg Lemond's spectacular victory over Laurent Fignon.

The American won the time trial (for many years the fastest in the history of the race: 54.5 km/h over 24 km) and overtook the Frenchman in the overall standings to win that edition by just 8 seconds.

From that year on, all teams began to use it and the UCI regulated its use in road cycling.

In addition, the introduction of this handlebar was the precursor to a change in the cycling industry that, in a few years, focused on improving performance through aerodynamic development.

63

Felice Gimondi, one of the greatest in cycling.

Nicknamed "The Phoenix", Felice Gimondi was one
of the great figures of cycling in the sixties
and early seventies.

He was probably the biggest rival that Eddy Merckx
faced in his crushing and successful cycling career.

And that's saying something, considering Gimondi
was already a champion with two Giros and a
Tour under his belt when the phenomenon of
"The Cannibal" exploded.

Precisely, the first major challenge that Gimondi
had to face in his early years was knowing how
to manage his unexpected victory in the
1965 Tour de France.

It was his first year as a professional cyclist and
after a meritorious Giro d'Italia in which he already
reached the podium (3rd), he was supposed to rest,
but the last-minute withdrawal of a teammate
forced him to line up, and the surprise was on: The
Phoenix became one of the youngest winners
of the Tour at only 23 years old.

64

In the Tour de France, there are over 4,500 workers.

It is estimated that an average of 12,000 fans travel to the sides of the French roads to watch the race, but in the mountain stages, there are many more.

The average TV audience of the French race is 12.7 million viewers.

There were 21 cyclists who completed the route of the first edition, although 60 riders started because each of the six stages of that first Tour de France had an average of 400 km.

The lowest average speed recorded in the history of the Tour was 24.05 km/h, precisely in 1919.

65

The tourist or Routier cyclist category remained in force in the early decades of the Tour de France, from its creation in 1903 until the late 1920s.

Cyclists in this category were considered amateurs and did not have the right to support teams; they had to be self-sufficient in everything.

They were often cyclists who were not professionals and participated in the race purely out of a passion for cycling and the challenge posed by the race.

Unlike professional cyclists who competed for sponsored teams and had access to support vehicles and mechanics, tourists or Routiers had to carry everything necessary to complete the race, from tools and spare parts to food and clothing.

Additionally, they had to repair their own bicycles and face adverse weather conditions.

Despite the difficulties, many tourist cyclists managed to complete the Tour de France and, in some cases, even win stages.

These cyclists were highly respected for their courage and determination and were considered true heroes of cycling.

Over the years, the tourist or Routier cyclist category disappeared from the Tour de France as the race became more professionalized and increasingly commercialized.

However, its legacy endures as a testament to the spirit of adventure and sacrifice involved in long-distance cycling and as an inspiration for amateur cyclists around the world.

66

In the Tour de France, jerseys or maillots are an important part of the race's identity and the achievements of the cyclists.

The yellow jersey is the most famous and distinguishes the leader of the overall classification of the race.

But in 1953, the green jersey was created to distinguish the winner by points or regularity, and in 1975, the polka dot jersey was created to distinguish the leader of the mountain classification.

The green jersey was created in 1953 to recognize the most consistent rider in the race, the one who earns points in each stage based on their final classification and the points awarded in intermediate sprints.

The green jersey has changed its design several times over the years, but has always maintained its green color.

The polka dot jersey was created in 1975 to recognize the best climber of the race, the one who accumulates points based on their classification in the mountain passes.

The design of the polka dot jersey was created by the sponsor Chocolat Poulain, and its striking white and red stripe design has remained until now.

Also in 1975, the white jersey was created to distinguish the best young rider in the race, the one who leads the overall classification and is under 26 years old.

This jersey was created in honor of the first young rider to win the race, the Frenchman Laurent Fignon.

The design of the white jersey has changed slightly over the years, but has always maintained its white color and distinctive blue collar and sleeves.

These jerseys are a fundamental part of the identity and tradition of the Tour de France, and are highly valued by the cyclists who compete in the race.

67

Henri Cornet was born on August 4, 1884 in the city of Desvres, France.

He began competing in cycling races at a very young age and his victory in the 1904 Tour de France made him a legend of French cycling.

His victory was very controversial, as it was rumored that he had received help from a car during a stage, but nothing was ever proven.

After winning the Tour de France, Cornet continued racing for several more years, but never again reached the glory he had achieved at 19 years old.

He participated in the Tour de France 10 times, finishing in the Top 10 in five of them, and won the prestigious Paris-Roubaix race in 1906.

Cornet retired from professional cycling in 1913 and during World War I, served as a messenger for the French army.

It should be noted that he was captured by the Germans and spent several years in prisoner of war camps.

After the war, he worked in the cycling industry as a race organizer and journalist.

Henri Cornet died on March 18, 1941 in Villejuif, France, at the age of 56.

His name is still remembered in the world of cycling as one of the great champions in the history of the Tour de France.

68

The Yellow Jersey is the most coveted prize of the Tour de France and is awarded to the rider who leads the general classification of the race.

The wearer of the Yellow Jersey receives a cash prize of 500 euros for each stage in which they wear it.

In addition, the winner of the Tour de France receives a cash prize of 500,000 euros.

Economic prizes in professional cycling are an important form of recognition for cyclists for their effort and dedication in the competition.

Additionally, the winner of the Tour de France receives other prizes and recognitions, such as the prestigious Tour de France trophy and fame and recognition in the world of cycling.

69

Why is the leader's jersey of the Tour de France yellow?

Legend gives an easy answer to this question by saying that yellow was the color of the L'Auto newspaper that organized the race, but history poses a slightly more elaborate explanation.

According to the official version, the first edition of the Tour de France in which the yellow jersey was used to distinguish the first-placed rider was in 1919.

The race was born in 1903, but was interrupted during the course of the Great War and was resumed precisely in 1919, when there had already been 11 editions.

The garment was created at the request of journalists who followed the race; they needed to quickly distinguish the first-placed rider.

70

The "bidon" breakaway.

Breakaways allowed by the peloton
have had unexpected prominence
in some Grand Tours.

The "bidon" breakaway is a breakaway of
several riders allowed by the peloton,
which manages to reach the finish line
with many minutes of advantage
over the main peloton.

Usually, the riders in the breakaway are not
relevant for the general classification, at
most, one of the members may wear the
leader's jersey in some stage, which
usually pleases the main favorites.

But this unwritten rule is not always
followed and, on occasion, that allowed
"bidon" breakaway becomes the most
important fact of the race, and even
decides the final winner.

71

**The 1956 Tour de France was very
exciting and full of surprises.**

The "bidon escape," which refers to a group of riders
who escape and drink water from bottles from
spectators instead of using official supply stations,
played a key role in the final outcome.

In the seventh stage, a group of 25 riders, including
Walkowiak and his podium companions Gilbert Bauvin
and Nello Lauredi, escaped and managed to
maintain their lead over the peloton.

The bidon escape became a legend of the Tour
de France and was the determining factor
in Walkowiak's victory.

The Frenchman, who had never won a major race
before, surprised himself and the cycling
world with his win.

Despite his victory, many fans and journalists criticized
his defensive and unspectacular cycling style, and the
French press even called him "the most unpopular
winner in the history of the Tour."

Despite this, Walkowiak always maintained his pride in
his victory and was a hero to cycling fans in his country.

72

**The 1990 Tour de France was very
exciting and unpredictable.**

In the first stage, a group of four riders (Frans Maassen,
Claudio Chiappucci, Ronan Pensec, and Steve Bauer)
managed to escape and gain a significant
lead over the peloton.

Steve Bauer became the first wearer of the yellow
jersey, but in the thirteenth stage, he handed it
over to Claudio Chiappucci, a relatively
unknown rider at that time.

Despite expectations that Chiappucci would soon cede
the lead, he managed to stay at the top and resist the
attacks of other top cyclists like Greg LeMond, Erik
Breukink, Pedro Delgado, and Marino Lejarreta.

Only in the final stage did LeMond manage to
surpass Chiappucci and win the Tour de France
for the second time in his career.

After his great performance in the 1990 Tour de France,
Chiappucci became a prominent rider in the Grand Tours,
obtaining podium finishes in the Giro d'Italia and Tour
de France and becoming one of Miguel Indurain's
main rivals in the 1990s.

73

The 2006 Tour de France edition was remembered for Óscar Pereiro's incredible comeback in the general classification thanks to his performance in stage 13, where he formed a breakaway with Jens Voigt and arrived at the finish line with more than 29 minutes of advantage over the peloton.

Pereiro managed to maintain this lead in the remaining mountain stages, allowing him to climb to second place in the general classification and eventually be declared the winner after then-leader Floyd Landis was disqualified for doping.

Pereiro and Voigt's bidon escape became one of the most famous in Tour de France history and is remembered as an example of the competitive spirit and determination of the riders.

74

Eddy Merckx is considered one of the greatest cyclists of all time, and holds several records in the Tour de France.

The Belgian led the race for a total of 96 stages, more than any other cyclist in the history of the competition.

In addition, he won a total of 34 stages, also a record in the Tour.

Merckx won the Tour de France five times, between 1969 and 1974, and also achieved the Giro d'Italia-Tour de France double in 1970.

His dominance on the road was such that he was nicknamed "The Cannibal" for his ability to devour his rivals in every race.

In addition to his victories in the Tour de France, Merckx also won a large number of important races, including the Road Cycling World Championship three times.

His professional career extended from 1965 to 1978, and he remains a legend of cycling to this day.

75

The Paris-Roubaix is a classic one-day cycling race, also known as the "Hell of the North" due to its very tough and rugged cobbled sections that riders must overcome.

The 2022 edition was won by Belgian rider Wout van Aert of the Jumbo-Visma team. The QuickStep Alpha Vinyl Team is a Belgian road cycling team, one of the most successful teams currently.

The bike they used in the 2022 Paris-Roubaix is the Specialized S-Works Roubaix, a high-end bike designed specifically for the race's conditions.

This bike features the adjustable front suspension system Future Shock 2.0, which helps dampen shocks and reduce rider fatigue.

The team uses prototype Roval tubeless wheels that have not yet been released to the market, along with prototype Specialized Project Black tires.

The tire width appears to be 30mm, which provides greater traction and comfort on cobbled sections.

To prevent the chain from coming off with the rattling of the cobbles, the bike uses a 54-46 chainring combination, which is not as common nowadays but is effective in this type of race.

Yves Lampaert's bike, a rider on the QuickStep Alpha Vinyl Team, has sandpaper on the stem cap, which acts as a dial to adjust the shock absorber's hardness.

This allows riders to adjust the suspension to their needs and preferences during the race.

76

**Dave Brailsford is a British cycling coach who
has been very successful in the sport.**

He became famous for leading the British track cycling
team at the 2004 Athens Olympics, where the team
won two gold medals, one silver, and one bronze.

He then became the general manager of the Sky road
cycling team in 2010, which later became the Ineos team.

Under Brailsford's leadership, the Sky/Ineos team won
numerous major cycling races, including the Tour
de France seven times, the Giro d'Italia twice,
and the Vuelta a España once.

His focus on "marginal gains," which focuses on optimizing
all aspects of a cyclist's performance, including training,
nutrition, technology, and equipment, has been
widely recognized as a key to his success.

In addition to his successes in competitive cycling,
Brailsford has been an advocate for fighting doping
in sports and has worked to promote ethical
practices in cycling.

He has been honored with several awards and
recognitions for his work in the sport, including
an appointment as Commander of the Order
of the British Empire in 2013.

77

Paolo Slongo is an Italian cycling coach who has worked with some of the best cyclists in his country, including Vincenzo Nibali, Ivan Basso, and Damiano Cunego.

He has been Nibali's coach for many years and played a key role in his victories in major tours, including the Tour de France, Giro d'Italia, and Vuelta a España.

Slongo is known for his rigorous and disciplined approach to training, and he has developed a customized training system for each of his riders.

His approach is based on training intensity and volume, as well as the importance of proper recovery and nutrition.

Slongo has also worked as a cycling commentator for Italian television and has written several books on cycling training and sports nutrition.

In summary, he is a highly respected coach in the world of cycling, and his success with some of the best Italian cyclists demonstrates his expertise and skill in coaching elite cyclists.

78

Tim Kerrison is an Australian coach who has worked with several elite cycling teams.

Prior to his career in cycling, Kerrison served as a sports scientist at the Australian Institute of Sport, where he worked with high-performance athletes in different sports.

Kerrison began working in cycling in 2005 as the coach of the Australian track team, where he contributed to the team's improved performance at the 2008 Beijing Olympics.

He later joined the Sky/Ineos team in 2010 as a performance coach, where he played a key role in the team's success at the Tour de France.

Kerrison is known for his focus on sports science and his ability to apply advanced training techniques in cycling.

He has been credited for his role in developing high-intensity training techniques and the application of sleep science in cyclist training.

In addition to working with cycling teams, Kerrison has also worked with athletes from other sports, including Australian swimmer Ian Thorpe, who won five gold medals at the 2000 Sydney and 2004 Athens Olympics.

79

Bobby Julich is a former American professional cyclist who has transitioned into coaching after retiring.

During his career as a cyclist, he competed in races such as the Tour de France, the Vuelta a España, and the Giro d'Italia, achieving several podium finishes in stages and one-day races.

After retiring, Julich started working as a coach, first with the Tinkoff-Saxo team and later with the BMC team.

With the Tinkoff-Saxo team, Julich worked with cyclists such as Alberto Contador, Peter Sagan, and Roman Kreuziger, while with the BMC team, he worked with cyclists such as Tejay van Garderen and Cadel Evans.

In addition to his work as a team coach, Julich has also worked as a personal coach for several cyclists, including Chris Horner, Levi Leipheimer, and George Hincapie.

Throughout his coaching career, he has helped his cyclists win major races, such as stages of the Tour de France and the Vuelta a España.

80

Dan Lorang is a German sports coach known for his work as the coach of the Bora-Hansgrohe cycling team and for working with some of the most successful cyclists in the world, including Peter Sagan and Emanuel Buchmann.

Lorang graduated in Sports Science from the University of Saarland and obtained a master's degree in Sports Science from the University of Leipzig.

He has also worked as a university professor of Sports Science at the University of Saarland and has published several research articles in the field of sports training.

In 2014, Lorang was hired as the coach of the Bora-Argon 18 team, which later became Bora-Hansgrohe in 2017.

Since then, he has helped the team achieve many notable achievements, including victories in stages of the Tour de France, the Giro d'Italia, and the Vuelta a España.

In addition to his work with the Bora-Hansgrohe team, Lorang has also worked with individual cyclists, such as Peter Sagan, the three-time road cycling world champion and one of the most successful cyclists today.

Lorang has been credited with helping Sagan improve his racing technique and reach his full potential as a cyclist.

Lorang has also worked with Emanuel Buchmann, a German cyclist who has had success in stage races around the world.

Lorang has helped Buchmann improve his climbing ability and become a stronger competitor in long-distance races.

81

Neal Henderson is an American cycling coach known for his work with some of the world's most successful cyclists, including Taylor Phinney, Rohan Dennis, and Evelyn Stevens.

He has also worked with the United States track cycling team.

Henderson is the founder of APEX Coaching, a sports training company based in Colorado.

He has been a cycling coach for over 20 years and has worked with cyclists of all levels, from beginners to Olympic cyclists and world champions.

Among the most successful cyclists Henderson has coached are Taylor Phinney, an American cyclist who has won several medals in world championships and has competed in the Tour de France, and Rohan Dennis, an Australian cyclist who has won several medals in world championships and has set several records in time trials.

Henderson also worked with Evelyn Stevens, an American cyclist who set the women's hour world record in 2016.

Stevens was coached by Henderson for much of her career and credits much of her success to his training approach.

In addition to his work with individual cyclists, Henderson has also worked with the United States track cycling team.

He was the head coach of the team at the 2015 Pan American Games and was an assistant coach for the team at the 2016 Rio Olympics.

82

Aldo Sassi was an Italian cycling coach who specialized in training cyclists for mountain races.

Sassi was the founder and director of the Mapei Sport Center, an elite training center for cyclists in Italy.

Sassi was a highly respected coach in the professional cycling world and worked with some of the most successful cyclists of his time, including Ivan Basso and Cadel Evans.

During his career, Sassi was known for his innovative approach to training cyclists to compete in mountain races.

He believed that proper training and nutrition were essential to the success of cyclists in high mountain races.

Under Sassi's guidance, Ivan Basso won the Giro d'Italia in 2006, and Cadel Evans won the Road Cycling World Championship in 2009.

Sassi also trained other notable cyclists such as Danilo Di Luca and Franco Pellizotti.

In addition to his work as a coach, Sassi was an advocate for clean sport in cycling and spoke publicly about the need to eradicate doping in the sport.

He was known for his tireless work ethic and commitment to the success of his cyclists.

Sassi passed away in 2010 at the age of 51 after a long battle with cancer.

However, his legacy as a coach and advocate for clean sport in cycling continues to be remembered and honored in the cycling community.

83

Iñigo San Millán is a Spanish sports physiologist who has worked as a consultant for several elite cycling teams, including the Trek-Segafredo team.

San Millán is known for his innovative approach to cyclist training and his expertise in data analysis and exercise physiology.

San Millán began his career in the cycling world as a coach and physiologist for several professional teams in Spain.

During this time, he worked with cyclists such as Alberto Contador, Fabian Cancellara, and Bauke Mollema, and helped design personalized training programs for each cyclist.

Later, San Millán joined the Trek-Segafredo team as a sports physiologist in 2017, where he worked with cyclists such as Alberto Contador and Bauke Mollema.

His work with the team focused on data analysis and identifying areas of improvement for each individual cyclist.

San Millán is known for his innovative approach to cyclist training and his use of advanced technology to maximize cyclists' performance.

His work has focused on physiological data analysis and understanding how the human body responds to exercise and training.

84

**Virtual cycling races:
The new modality in e-sports.**

The World Cycling Champion, Norwegian
Mads Pedersen from Trek-Segafredo,
participated with 19 other teammates
in the first World Tour Virtual
test on April 22, 2020.

Faced with the mandatory cycling break
due to the Covid 19 pandemic, a few
bright minds, taking advantage of the
opportunities offered for a long time by
the platforms that power smart roller
training sessions, have started organizing
slightly more serious challenges within
what is already known as E-sports.

85

How have virtual cycling races been forged?

The first was the 2020 Milan San Remo Virtual, a challenge organized by Garmin and open to the public.

On March 21, 4,221 participants faced a virtual route of 57km, which reproduced the terrain gradients on their rollers, altering the resistance.

This was followed by the first round of the Tour of Flanders, the already mythical Ronde Van Vlaanderen, but this time the organization invited 13 professionals.

The news is that the software used in this race is from the Spanish company Bkool.

The race would be won by Greg Van Avermaet.

86

Digital Swiss 5 is the first virtual professional cycling tour in history.

There will be a before and after Digital Swiss 5; here the experiments end, and we will witness the first virtual race in professional cycling history, emulating the UCI World Tour with 19 professional teams invited.

Everything is a virtual replica: 5 stages in 5 days, real sponsors, team strategies (directors can present different lineups each day and give instructions as the stage progresses).

The event is organized by Velon and the Tour de Suisse using software from the Czech manufacturer Rouvy.

The Rouvy platform has the novelty that an intelligent training roller is not necessary, it can be used with a traditional roller.

To connect, only an ANT+ sensor and an Android, IOS mobile device or PC are needed and the application downloaded.

87

The first race of Digital Swiss 5 consisted of 5 stages in total.

Each stage presented different characteristics
and challenges for the cyclists.

The characteristics of each stage are detailed below:

- **Stage 1:** Moudon-Leukerbad - 26.6 km in length, with a
positive gradient of 1,192 meters. It was a mountainous and
challenging stage that required good climbing resistance.

- **Stage 2:** Frauenfeld-Frauenfeld - 46 km in length, with a
positive gradient of 180 meters. This stage was flatter and
faster, with some technical sections that required skillful
riding.

- **Stage 3:** Fiesch-Disentis-Sedrun (Nufenen Pass) - 33.1 km
in length, with a positive gradient of 1,512 meters. It was
another mountainous and challenging stage, with a long
climb through the Nufenen Pass.

- **Stage 4:** Oberlangenegg-Lagnau Emmental - 36.8 km in
length, with a positive gradient of 444 meters. This stage
had a smoother altimetry profile compared to the first two,
but still required some skill to maintain pace through the
rolling terrain.

- **Stage 5:** Fiesch-Disentis-Sedrun (Lukmanier Pass) - 36 km
in length, with a positive gradient of 950 meters. It was the
last stage of the race and presented another demanding
climb through the Lukmanier Pass.

88

Cyclocross: the toughest cycling.

Talking about cyclocross (CX) is thinking
about "road" bikes covered in mud.

But something has completely turned around
"that dingy cyclocross" and turned it
into the trendiest discipline in cycling.

An intervention by the best advertisers and
designers in the bicycle industry, coupled
with races with really substantial cash prizes,
along with global television coverage, have
transformed the forgotten discipline of cycling
into the center of attention for cycling
fans, specialized press and each
and every manufacturer.

The epicenter of this discipline globally is
located in Belgium, where one of its Grand Prix
races can attract up to 60,000 spectators,
who have previously paid up to €20
to access the circuit.

89

What are CX bikes like?

There are many differences with Gravel:

-Gravel: Leisure. Riding on forest tracks, without obstacles and without sandy or muddy traps.

-Cyclocross: Competition or Training. Riding on circuits, often off-road, and with impossible slopes, steps, sandy areas and muddy areas, which require alternating with running on foot.

A CX bike has the following characteristics:

The base, that is, the frame, is optimized to ride on uneven terrain:

-Greater distance between axles: greater stability.

-Greater bottom bracket height: prevents pedals from hitting the ground.

-Greater width in chainstays and fork legs: allows wider tires to be mounted.

-More relaxed head tube angle: allows for larger steps to be taken.

90

Bikepacking is "the latest" in cycle-tourism.

It consists of combining mountain biking with the basic principles of long-distance hiking and camping.

These are the keys to bikepacking:

-Preferably use forest tracks and trails. Routes are planned to venture into nature.

-Self-sufficiency is the second premise. A bikepacker carries everything to camp, cook, and sleep on their bicycle.

-Standard panniers in traditional cycle-tourism are not useful in this discipline because they destabilize the bicycle on very technical routes. They are replaced by special bags that are attached to parts of the frame and the bike and center the weight.

91

What are Bikepacking bikes like?

There are no ideal bikes for Bikepacking, as this type of activity has as many interpretations as there are practitioners.

Some prefer to travel very lightly and carry everything in a backpack on a gravel bike, while others opt for a MTB with Plus wheels, as they plan to cross a true hell.

Features include: a larger front triangle to allow the use of large frame bags, inverted stems resulting from a longer than usual steering tube to build the large triangle, road handlebars or multi-position bars that allow riders to place their hands in different positions and rest, up to 3 water bottle mounts, and rigid forks as suspension forks with the heavy load of the bikes don't work, at least for small impacts.

92

For efficient transportation: Commuter.

It is a bike with a steering angle
designed for slow turns at 90 degrees,
and a higher bottom bracket to avoid
hitting the ground if you pedal
by mistake while turning.

They come with all the necessary
mounts for fenders and racks.

The handlebar gives you a more
upright posture, which expands
your field of vision.

Chain guards are common to
avoid dirtying your pants.

The real comfort cruiser bikes: Comfort.

They are distinguished by an upright
pedaling posture, a wider saddle,
and a comfortable grip handlebar.

Some manufacturers offer a curved top
tube that is as close to the ground as
possible, making it very easy to
get on and off the bike.

Electra incorporates all of the above and
adds its own technology called Flat Foot
Geometry, which essentially means that you
can stand at a stoplight and touch the
ground with both feet, but when pedaling,
you can fully extend your leg.

94

Minimalism on wheels: Fixed.

A Fixed or Fixie bike comes from the bikes used on velodromes and has two unmistakable characteristics:

- A fixed gear, meaning you pedal forward to move forward and pedal backward to go in reverse, and no brakes.

- To stop the bike, you use the strength of your legs to slow down the pedaling.

Initially used by bike messengers for its low maintenance cost, it was later adopted by urban cycling tribes as an exercise in "posturing" first and a lifestyle second.

You can use them for commuting, but they are neither the most efficient nor the most comfortable.

Remember that there are no gears, so you'll expend a lot of energy on any ride, and there are no brakes, so you'll have to rely heavily on your vision and hearing.

95

Space-saving and combined transportation: Folding bikes.

Folding bikes can fold onto themselves several times in a matter of seconds and, once assembled, allow you to travel at a considerable speed.

Initially designed as bikes to take on recreational boats, they ended up being a very useful tool in the city.

Whether it's because of space constraints or for practical reasons when combining public transport with biking, folding bikes have become a popular choice among urban cyclists.

Two manufacturers that clearly lead in this sector are Brompton and Dahon.

The key is in the solidity of their closures, a real scourge for most manufacturers of this type of bike, and an insurmountable problem (due to cost) for those produced by large retailers and premium finishes.

96

Ebikes are electric bicycles that use an electric motor to provide pedal assistance.

These bikes have become increasingly popular in recent years because they allow cyclists to travel longer distances and climb steep hills more easily.

According to the regulations of the European Community (CE), Ebikes must meet certain characteristics to be considered bikes with assisted pedaling.

The electric motor must not exceed 250 W, and the maximum speed of the bike must be 25 km/h.

If the bike's speed exceeds 25 km/h, the motor will stop working, and the bike will operate solely on the cyclist's pedaling force.

In addition, Ebikes cannot weigh more than 40 kg and must comply with other safety requirements, such as adequate brakes, lighting, and signaling.

These bikes are a more environmentally friendly and economical alternative to motor vehicles and can be used for both leisure trips and daily commuting.

4 reasons to use an Ebike.

- Matching physical fitness. If for whatever reason you can't keep up with your group, or can't climb certain hills, luckily you don't have to give up cycling. An Ebike helps you keep up with the rest of the group and allows you to continue enjoying your favorite activity.

- Commute without sweating. You can cycle to work without breaking a sweat. You're not looking for exercise, you're looking for transportation.

- Ecology. Move around the city without consuming resources. Save parking space, avoid traffic jams, and reduce CO_2 emissions.

- Climb impossible hills. If you can't climb it, it's because you've flipped over. The assistance of an electric motor is sufficient to overcome any hill (except a trial), and at a constant speed.

98

Ebike. Characteristics of the Bosch motor.

The German manufacturer Bosch has produced, according to experts, the best assisted pedaling system for electric mountain bikes: Bosch Performance CX.

A motor capable of providing 300% assistance (the motor multiplies your pedaling force by three).

The Performance CX distributes its performance in 4 levels of assistance:

- Turbo and you'll have a 300% boost.

- Sport gives you 210%.

- Tour with 120%.

- Eco with 50% You control the power and battery charge as needed.

The announced autonomy is between 30 and 160 kilometers, depending on the power mode, terrain, and other conditions.

And to charge it, simply plug it into a conventional power outlet and wait between 3 and 5 hours to complete the charge.

99

Accessories for urban cycling.

- **Helmet:** once again, you don't need a special city helmet. But remember that they exist, and there are also models specifically designed for women.

- **Lights:** some bikes come equipped with lights, but if not, don't forget to buy a rear and front light. Apart from safety, this is also required by the General Traffic Regulations.

- **Lock:** don't skimp on the lock. They can be as cheap as 6€, but you know how much your bike is worth.

- **Rack:** a rack is a very practical accessory when cycling in the city. It allows you to unload all the weight from your body and carry large packages.

- **Waterproof clothing:** if in Denmark they only used bikes on dry days, they wouldn't even reach 50 days a year...the trick is to have the right clothing.

- **Shoulder bag:** to avoid sweating on your back, don't use a backpack. Use a shoulder bag.

100

Soft Tail systems are a technology applied to mountain bike frames that provide greater comfort and traction for the rider.

Unlike full suspension frames, Soft Tail systems only flex slightly in the rear triangle to provide minimal suspension without adding extra weight or interfering with pedaling.

This flex is achieved through frame design and the choice of appropriate materials to provide just the right amount of flexibility in the rear stays.

Travel is usually very short, around 3-4 cm, and suspension is provided by the frame's own flexing, without additional pivot points between the stays and the bottom bracket.

Soft Tail technology is a popular choice for XC (cross country) riders seeking greater comfort and control on difficult terrain without compromising performance or speed.

101

A sticker brand is a company that purchases pre-made bicycle frames from an Asian manufacturer and simply adds its own decoration, logo, and branding to market it as its own product.

This process is known as OEM (Original Equipment Manufacturer) and is common in the bicycle industry.

The problem with sticker brands is that there is often inadequate quality control, which means that the frames may not have the proper thickness and material bonding, compromising the safety and durability of the bike.

Additionally, the frame may not offer the desired traction on climbs, stability on descents, or good cornering.

Another issue is that these brands often are not transparent about the origin of the frame and the manufacturer, making it difficult for end consumers to make an informed decision about the quality of the product they are buying.

Therefore, it is important to research before buying a bike from a sticker brand and make sure that the frame and components are of high quality and built to last.

If you have enjoyed the cycling curiosities presented in this book, we would like to ask you to share a review on Amazon.

Your opinion is extremely valuable to us and to other cycling enthusiasts who are looking to be entertained and learn new knowledge.

We understand that leaving a comment can be a tedious process, but we kindly ask you to take a few minutes of your time to share your thoughts and opinions with us.

Your support is highly important to us and it helps us continue creating quality content for lovers of this incredible sport.

We appreciate your support in advance.

★ ★ ★ ★ ★